MEDIEVAL LIFE

BY

JOHN GUY

COUNTRY LIFE

*T*he lives of medieval peasants were inextricably linked to the natural cycle, to the weather and to the rhythm of the seasons. They went to bed when the light faded, and rose early with the sun. Most families rented a small strip of land in the large open fields, paying a percentage of the yield to the lord or church as a tax called a tithe. Most of the work was done by hand.

TREADING THE GRAPES

Many medieval communities had small vineyards. Grapes were harvested in the late summer, and wine pressing was performed in September by treading the grapes in large vats.

HURDLES

Wattle hurdles, made from hazel, were mostly used to fence in livestock. Posts were driven into the ground and interwoven with a mixture of rounded and split strips of wood.

THE MILLER'S TALE

Millers were not popular figures in medieval society. Tenant farmers were forced to use their lord's mill and pay whatever he demanded. The English writer Geoffrey Chaucer wrote a scathing attack on the profession in his famous Canterbury Tales, written between 1380–1392.

THRESHING

After harvesting wheat, the corn was threshed. The grain was separated by beating the straw using an early tool called a jointed wooden flail.

SUPPLEMENTING THE DIET

For the poor, supplementing the diet by hunting wild animals on common land was essential, but if they were caught poaching on the lord's estate they would be severely punished. Persistent offenders might even be executed. This poacher is nervously looking over his shoulder as he steals a bird.

FOWLING

For youths from wealthy families, fowling provided good archery practice. A dog was used to fetch any birds shot and brought to the ground. When proficient, the youths progressed to hawking or hunting with their fathers.

SHEEP SHEARING

Much of the wealth of the Middle Ages was founded on the wool trade. Most families participated in sheep shearing in June, using hand shears.

LIFE IN TOWNS

*T*he medieval economy was based largely on land ownership. A complex hierarchy of tenancy existed, with most of the wealthier barons living on their estates. As the Middle Ages progressed, however, more crafts and support trades were required. These people did not work the land but sold their services, so they tended to congregate where the markets were held. Houses were built lining the roads leading to the market, forming the nucleus of a town. Conditions were often cramped and unhygienic and there was always the risk of fire because the houses were made of timber and thatch. The larger towns were allowed to form councils and become self-governing.

THE MARKET PLACE

At the centre of every town was the market place. It was usually situated at a crossroads, where merchants gathered to sell or exchange their wares. Goods were transported from neighbouring villages by packhorse or cart.

WALLED CITIES

The more important towns were surrounded by defensive walls, though this was more for prestige than because of any real threat. Occasionally, towns were besieged and each citizen would be expected to defend the walls to prevent the town being over-run or razed to the ground.

SANITATION

Sanitation was a major problem in medieval towns. Drainage ditches ran alongside the streets, but these became open sewers if not regularly cleaned. When this happened, ditches would become infested with rats, allowing disease to spread.

POPULATION

Only 5% of the population lived in towns. With the exception of large cities, such as London or York, most towns were quite small, with an average population of only 500.

WATER TRANSPORT

Because of the poor state of the roads, towns were sited on rivers or the coast to facilitate transport. Here a barge is being loaded with goods for export.

COUNTRY TOWNS

Most country towns were little more than large villages. Many of the inhabitants still farmed the surrounding land. Others might be merchants or tradespeople who tended a small plot alongside their house to provide extra food or extra income, which is the origin of modern-day allotment gardens.

THE POOR AT HOME

EARLY CANDLES

Candles, made from melted animal fat, were the only source of artificial light.

The majority of people in medieval times lived in rural communities and worked on the land. Any excess food produced was sold at markets to supply townspeople and professional folk. Among the poor, bartering was very common, with goods and services being mutually exchanged without money changing hands. Few owned their own houses. Instead they rented them from the lord or the church. Living conditions were spartan, with the whole family sharing just one room.

BABES IN ARMS

When travelling on foot, babies were carried either in baskets suspended on the shoulder (left), or in a kind of haversack on the back (right).

SUBSISTENCE FARMING

Wool from sheep and goats was used to make clothes. Any excess was sold off at market. Dairy cows were a valuable source of milk nourishment and not generally slaughtered in the winter cull.

A WORTHY TRADE

Most people from the poorer classes had to work on the land.
One of the few exceptions were smiths. They forged metal ores, shoed
horses and made and repaired tools, so their work was always
in demand. Their forges were fuelled by coal and
usually built of stone because of the fire risk.

THE ANNUAL CULL

Winter fodder was in short supply
so animals were slaughtered each
November to provide food for
the cold months ahead.

POTTERY CONTAINERS

For the poor, most
tableware consisted
of pottery jars and
bowls, made locally
in small kilns.
Shown here is
a 14th century
serving jug.
Flat pieces
of bread
were used
instead of
plates. They
soaked up any
juices and were
then eaten.

KEEPING WARM

Houses had an
open hearth in the
centre of the room.
Peasants were
allowed to
gather bundles
of fallen timber
from nearby
common land
to use as fuel.

LIFE FOR THE RICH

By the late middle ages most of the nobility could read and write, many in Latin as well as English. The above inkwells are late medieval.

*T*he most striking thing that we would have noticed about domestic life in the Middle Ages, even for the rich, would have been the general lack of privacy. Much of daily life (including administrative and judicial matters) was carried out in the hall, which acted as a communal dining and living room. The level of domestic comfort was quite high, with ample provision of fireplaces. Internal walls were brightly decorated and windows were often glazed. Lighting was by candle or oil lamp.

A STATUS SYMBOL

Much of the tableware used by the rich was made of metal, such as silver or pewter. This gilt engraved chalice dates from the mid-13th century. Nobles considered that pottery and earthenware should only be used by the lower classes.

PREFERENTIAL TREATMENT

In most rich families only boys received a formal education. Girls were instructed at home in domestic duties, such as embroidery. Many were literate and would recite passages from the Bible or epic stories to entertain their families.

PRIDE OF THE TABLE

The rich ate very well. Meals consisted of 10 or more courses. Royal banquets might extend to several hundred courses! Food was often decorated, or disguised, after cooking. For example, feathers would be pushed back into a pheasant to make the dish resemble the live bird.

SWEET MUSIC

Evening meals lasted several hours and were often accompanied by musicians. Jesters, jugglers and acrobats might entertain between courses.

THE BARON'S HALL

The magnificent great hall at Penshurst Place, Kent, was built in the 14th century. It was 62 ft long, 39 ft wide and 60 ft high. Life-size carved figures supported the roof braces.

SONGBIRDS

Caged songbirds, such as linnets or finches, were popular in wealthy households, kept in cane or wicker cages. Regarded more as a decorative feature than as pets, they were usually found in ladies' quarters.

FOOD & DRINK

There was no shortage of variety in the food eaten at a lord's table. It might include beef, mutton, pork, poultry (or other birds such as starlings, pigeons, or gulls) vegetables, fruit, cheese, soup, fish, herbal salads and bread, followed by ale or wine. Hot herbal infusions were often enjoyed at the table. Diet for the poorer classes was more basic and probably comprised of more vegetables and stews, and less meat. Knives and spoons were the only cutlery used.

FOOD PRESERVATION

Salting, smoking and hanging were the only ways to preserve meat, which was often eaten immediately after slaughtering.

A SWEET TOOTH

Honey was used as sweetener in medieval times. Bees (then regarded as birds, not insects) were kept in wicker or wooden hives in a raised shelter as protection against vermin and the weather.

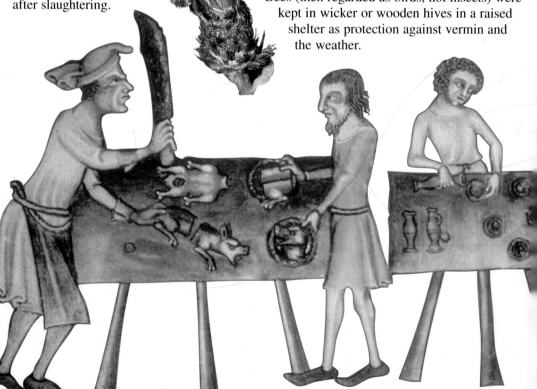

COOKING POTS

Food was generally cooked in large, open fireplaces. Pots, such as this 14th-century bronze skillet with legs, were placed right in the flames to ensure the food was thoroughly cooked.

THE BAKER'S OVEN

This medieval scene shows a baker preparing bread in an oven. Bread was made from whole-wheat flour and had a stodgy consistency.

SOMETHING FISHY

The Church forbade the eating of meat during Lent, so a medieval diet was supplemented by fish. Most great houses and villages had a pond (or river) nearby for this purpose, ever mindful of the power of the Church.

THE SPICE OF LIFE

Spices such as ginger, cinnamon, pepper and cloves were imported from the Middle East to disguise the flavour of bad or rancid food.

PREPARING THE FOOD

This illustration shows suckling pigs being prepared for serving at a lord's table. Food was prepared in a separate building or if weather permitted, outside, because of the fire risk.

PASTIMES

JACK-IN-THE-GREEN

This engraving of Penshurst Place shows a mummer's play being performed as part of the Christmas festivities. The basic theme is life triumphing over death or good over evil, and is the origin of modern-day pantomimes.

Medieval people took every opportunity to relax after work and engage in pastimes for entertainment or sport. Many of these games we would still recognise, such as chess, football and hockey. Combat sports were popular too. There were several public holidays (some religious, some linked to rural festivals) when the whole community would celebrate.

THE TOURNEY

Knights practised their skills by taking part in jousts (using lances) or tourneys (using swords and maces). The weapons were blunted and intended only to unseat the rider, but accidents were common, sometimes resulting in death.

MUSIC & DANCE

Life was not all drudgery and whenever they could, rich and poor people alike would engage in merrymaking. Formation dancing (similar to modern country dancing) was popular. Typical instruments were bagpipes, flutes, trumpets, lutes and hand drums.

A-HUNTING WE WILL GO

For the rich, hawking and hunting with dogs were popular pursuits.
They became great social events and even ladies took part, as shown here.

FAIRS

Although principally intended for merchants to sell their wares, fares attracted large numbers of entertainers. The stilt walker here, along with jugglers, jesters and musicians, would have been a familiar sight.

CHILDREN'S GAMES

These children are playing a version of hockey.
The ball is probably made from an animal's bladder.

FASHION

*I*n the early medieval period there was surprisingly little difference between the clothes worn by men and women. Both wore several layers of garments. The outer ones were loose fitting to allow for mobility, whilst retaining warmth. Undergarments usually consisted of leggings and vests, with tunics and wrap-around cloaks over the top. By the end of the Middle Ages the design of clothes was no longer governed by practical considerations, but often for the sake of fashion. Many of the garments were probably uncomfortable to wear, with the emphasis (at least for the rich) on the design and fabrics used.

NATURAL COLOURS

Most fabrics used in making clothes were of wool or linen. Each piece of material was usually dyed a single colour using natural plant extracts, such as woad, which produced a blue dye.

SOCIAL STANDING

The length of a person's over-tunic (cotte) showed their status. Poor people wore them to the knee; merchants to the calf; clergy and professional classes to the ankle.

HIGH SOCIETY

The wealthy spent a lot of money on clothes. Women wore long flowing dresses, while men wore leggings and over-tunics. Cloaks were the usual form of outer garment.

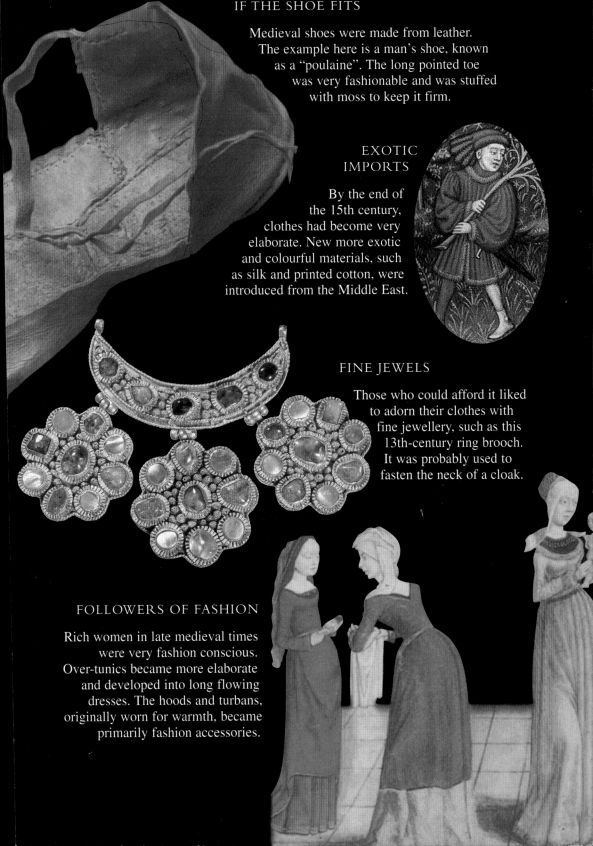

IF THE SHOE FITS

Medieval shoes were made from leather.
The example here is a man's shoe, known
as a "poulaine". The long pointed toe
was very fashionable and was stuffed
with moss to keep it firm.

EXOTIC IMPORTS

By the end of
the 15th century,
clothes had become very
elaborate. New more exotic
and colourful materials, such
as silk and printed cotton, were
introduced from the Middle East.

FINE JEWELS

Those who could afford it liked
to adorn their clothes with
fine jewellery, such as this
13th-century ring brooch.
It was probably used to
fasten the neck of a cloak.

FOLLOWERS OF FASHION

Rich women in late medieval times
were very fashion conscious.
Over-tunics became more elaborate
and developed into long flowing
dresses. The hoods and turbans,
originally worn for warmth, became
primarily fashion accessories.

ART & ARCHITECTURE

*T*he Middle Ages have left behind a legacy
of magnificent buildings and fine art treasures.
The technological advances made
in building techniques remain
unsurpassed, shown by the fact that
so many houses, churches and
castles have survived.
The illustrated
manuscripts, jewellery,
pottery, metalwork,
sculpture and carved
woodwork are just
some of the many
treasures from the
period. It was an age
astonishing for the
richness, beauty and
variety of its art; an
aspect of medieval life
too easily overlooked.

FINE ENAMEL

Not all medieval pottery
was crude earthenware,
as is popularly supposed.
This delightful vase depicts
two scenes of a hawking
party. The enamelled
work is quite exquisite.

THE MASON'S SKILLS

Bodiam Castle in Sussex was built in 1385. It is typical of a late medieval castle. By this time, castles were built by a much simpler, more regular design. Bodiam sits four square within a large moat, relying for its strength on lofty corner towers and a massive greenhouse. The lord's quarters were separate and defensible from within, as a precaution against treachery from mercenary soldiers.

EVERY PICTURE TELLS A STORY

Stained glass windows are one of the glories of medieval churches. This window dates from the 14th century. Before tracery was invented, windows were subdivided by iron bars. Lead strips separated each piece of coloured glass.

THE CRUCK OF THE MATTER

Most peasant houses were of cruck construction, with dirt floors and thatched roofs. The basic design was similar to a ridge tent, consisting of a series of timber A-frames connected along the ridge by a single joist.

RABID DOG

This rabid dog has just bitten the man on the right. The doctor is about to perform surgery. It was common to have a bird present at operations; if its appetite was good, it was an omen of recovery.

HEALTH & MEDICINE

S tandards of hygiene were higher than is popularly assumed. People bathed fairly regularly in wooden tubs and used herbal soaps and toothpaste. Monasteries and rich nobles installed piped water supplies and had flushable toilets, though these were exceptional. Some doctors attended university, but most were untrained. Herbal remedies were common (sold in apothecaries' shops), so too was blood-letting and urine diagnosis. Barbers performed dentistry and minor surgery.

LEPROSY

Beggars were a common sight in medieval towns, and many of them were lepers. Leprosy is caused by a microbe that infects the skin and nerves, causing ulcers, loss of sensation and ultimately, paralysis and loss of tissue. Although leprosy sufferers were made outcasts of society, only one form of the disease is actually infectious.

THE SURGEON'S KNIFE

The surgeon in this 14th-century illustration is about to perform an operation on the patient's eye. Whilst many medications were effective against minor ailments, the risk of infection following surgery was high, with a less than 50% success rate.

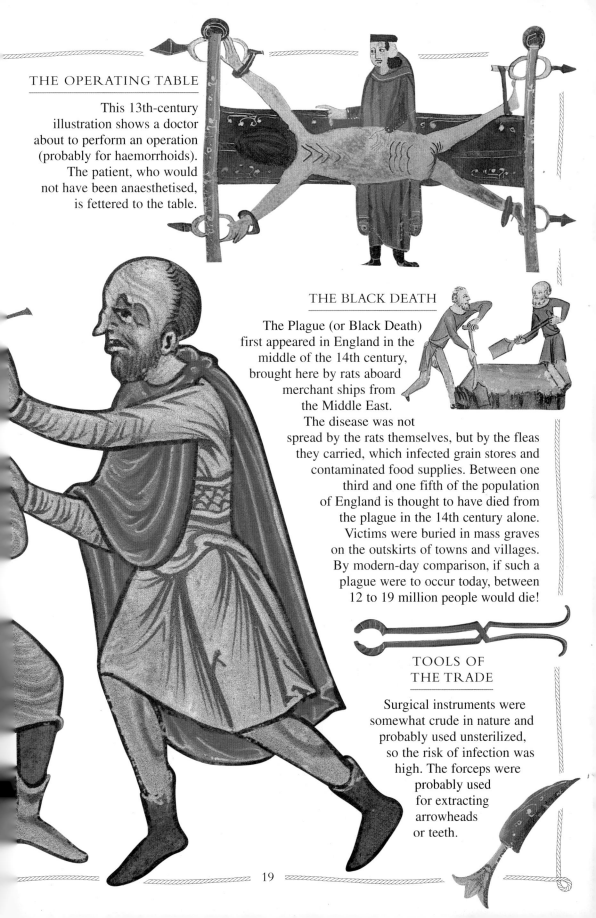

THE OPERATING TABLE

This 13th-century illustration shows a doctor about to perform an operation (probably for haemorrhoids). The patient, who would not have been anaesthetised, is fettered to the table.

THE BLACK DEATH

The Plague (or Black Death) first appeared in England in the middle of the 14th century, brought here by rats aboard merchant ships from the Middle East.

The disease was not spread by the rats themselves, but by the fleas they carried, which infected grain stores and contaminated food supplies. Between one third and one fifth of the population of England is thought to have died from the plague in the 14th century alone. Victims were buried in mass graves on the outskirts of towns and villages. By modern-day comparison, if such a plague were to occur today, between 12 to 19 million people would die!

TOOLS OF THE TRADE

Surgical instruments were somewhat crude in nature and probably used unsterilized, so the risk of infection was high. The forceps were probably used for extracting arrowheads or teeth.

LOVE & MARRIAGE

THE AGE OF ROMANCE

Gardens were frequently the setting for love matches. Young girls from aristocratic families were usually chaperoned by a woman servant at such meetings.

*M*arriages were often arranged by girls' fathers to secure an income or increase a family's wealth. For a peasant girl, whose father might not be a 'freeman' under feudal law, permission to marry had to be sought from the lord. Widows were often sent to convents and had their lands confiscated.

SPRING LOVERS

To the medieval mind, spring was the season of rebirth and a time to purge the body of winter's impurities. Amongst the recommended spring-time activities were blood-letting, bathing and making love!

A DANGEROUS ENGAGEMENT

During medieval times, knights became very popular, due in part to the publication of Thomas Malory's *Le Morte D'Arthur* in 1485. Knights, in chivalric armour, would sometimes fight at tournaments for the hand in marriage of a lady.

FORBIDDEN LOVE

Gay relationships were frowned upon during medieval times. Hugh Despenser, accused, among other things of a homosexual relationship with Edward II, was hung drawn and quartered for his crimes.

CHASTITY

Wives were expected to obey their husbands and remain faithful in their absence. To make sure they did, some were made to wear chastity belts. These were uncomfortable devices, which prevented them from making love.

CIRCLE OF HANDS

The dancers in this scene are performing a "carole", or ring dance. It was popular with young lovers because the dancers held hands, providing an opportunity for flirtation.

KING JOHN'S CHILD BRIDE

King John's second marriage was to Isabella of Angouleme, a girl barely in her teens. When his royal power was threatened by the impending marriage of Isabella to Hugh le Brun, John stopped it proceeding and married her himself, thus strengthening his position. He is said to have fallen passionately in love with her, spending so much time in her company that he ignored his kingly duties.

WOMEN & CHILDREN

ROCK-A-BYE-BABY

Although dating from the end of the medieval period, rocking cradles were widely used, showing a level of domestic comfort not generally realised.

The role of women and children in medieval society was considered secondary to that of men. There were few opportunities open to women and little chance of an education. For the wealthy there were usually just two choices – marriage or the nunnery. For the poor, the only option was work. Many marriages were arranged. Child brides were not uncommon, and most girls could expect to be married by the age of 14. Only the sons of the rich received an education and would usually be trained as soldiers or courtiers. Poor children worked in the fields or might be trained in their father's trade.

MIDWIFERY

Midwifery was one of the few occupations that might be termed a profession open to women. It was not uncommon for babies to be born by Caesarean section (so called because Julius Caesar was supposedly born by this operation), often performed after the mother had died during labour.

CLOTH MAKING

Most fabrics were made from wool and linen. Spinning and weaving were domestic chores usually undertaken by women in the house. Children helped with carding – untangling the raw fibre.

AN ENGLISHMAN'S HOME

The number of people who made up a castle's household could be surprisingly small. When under siege all available hands would be required to help defend the walls, including the women, whose fate if the castle fell was very unpleasant.

CHILD MORTALITY

This grim picture shows 'Death' claiming the life of a boy whilst playing. Life expectancy, was much lower than today. Death during childbirth was common for mother and baby alike. About 50% of children died before reaching age 20, especially among the poor.

CHILD'S PLAY

This late medieval illustration shows children playing blind-man's-buff and pick-a-back, simple games still played today.

WAR & WEAPONRY

Although castles were becoming increasingly fortified, invaders were developing increasingly sophisticated methods of gaining entry to these buildings. This siege tower would be brought alongside a wall and a drawbridge lowered onto the battlements.

*I*n early medieval times, kings and nobles raised armies under the provisions of the feudal system, whereby everyone was expected to provide military service if called upon. In the later Middle Ages, particularly after the black death which reduced the population considerably, professional soldiers were hired for a fee.

BESIEGED

The full horrors of medieval warfare are shown in this 13th century illustration. Ghastly wounds were inflicted and probably as many died from secondary infections afterwards as on the battlefield. The large sling-like contraption at the top of the picture is a trebuchet, a powerful machine capable of hurling huge boulders against a castle wall.

Crossbow

Longbow

THE ARCHER'S SKILL

In many ways the longbow was a superior weapon to the crossbow, much more effective at a long range and easier to load and fire in quick succession. The crossbow, however, was more powerful at close quarters and was particularly favoured by castle defenders.

THE NORMAN CONQUEST

This scene from the Bayeaux Tapestry shows the Battle of Hastings. Duke William's skilful use of archers and mounted knights eventually defeated Harold's foot soldiers.

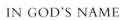

IN GOD'S NAME

Many of the atrocities committed in warfare were carried out in the Church's name. Here the God of Love blesses warriors going into battle.

SURRENDERING THE KEYS

Most sieges were resolved by negotiation, with adversaries outmanoeuvring one another, or by starving the defenders into submission. As a last resort, a military assault would ensue. The people in this view are surrendering the keys to the city after a successful siege.

CRIME & PUNISHMENT

*T*he popular notion of lawlessness in the Middle Ages is largely unfounded. Most petty crimes were tried through local courts, usually by the lord. More serious crimes were referred to sessional judges who toured the country four times a year. Shire reeves, or sheriffs, were responsible for keeping law and order. Prisons were a rarity, most crimes being punished by fines, compensation or death.

THE GALLOWS

Violent crimes like murder were punishable by death. However, a felony also included theft over one shilling. Execution was by beheading, burning or hanging.

THE ROYAL COURT

The Crown had overall control over the courts, although it took a direct interest only in serious crimes. Henry II first introduced the judicial circuit, when judges regularly toured the country, hearing cases.

THE PEASANTS' REVOLT

In 1381 the peasants, who had long suffered high taxation, revolted against the introduction of a new poll tax. Wat Tyler, one of the leaders, is seen here being slain in negotiations with Richard II, who afterwards quelled and dispersed the mob.

ST. AGATHA

Torture was reserved for political or religious crimes. It was often used to extract confessions. The unfortunate woman in the picture, St. Agatha, is about to have her breasts cut off by garrotting, a common method of torture in the Middle Ages. It is believed Agatha was a 6th century virgin martyr who died at the hands of Quintian, Roman governer of Sicily. He tried unsuccessfully to seduce her and persuade her to renounce her vows to Christ. Like most torture victims, she died from her injuries.

PUBLIC HUMILIATION

The poor were allowed to seek alms from the Church, but anyone caught begging was likely to be flogged or be put in the stocks as punishment.

FALL FROM GRACE

The knight in this picture, presumably found guilty of an offence, is bound and stripped of his armour. The humiliation of being paraded publicly through the streets in a cart was considered part of the punishment.

TRANSPORT & SCIENCE

onasteries were at the forefront of innovations in agriculture and medicine, but the rate of technological development was slow. The feudal system itself was a contributing factor and delayed the necessary investment in new technology. Ideas took time to evolve, thwarted by difficulties of transport and communication. Many roads were unmade and impassable in winter, and most towns relied on water-borne transport for trade.

MAKING FIRE

In the days before matches, the simple act of making fire was very inconvenient. Various techniques were employed, most using some form of friction to kindle dry wood, such as the whirling and drilling system shown here.

WATER POWER

The power of water was harnessed by using water wheels, placed in the flows of a fast-moving river. As the wheel turned, geared shafts conveyed the power to turn machinery or millstones.

WILLIAM CAXTON

Before the invention of printing, all books had to be handwritten, usually by monks or clerks. This process was extremely slow, so books could be afforded only by the rich. William Caxton introduced printing into England from the continent in the 1470s. The first books were in Latin, but he later specialised in English. Caxton's press made possible the mass production of books, bringing the written word to ordinary people for the first time and laying the foundations of modern literacy.

YOUR CARRIAGE AWAITS

Most travelling was done on horseback. Carts were used for transporting trade goods. Carriages, like this one, were usually reserved for royalty or rich nobles.

WATER TRANSPORT

These Norman ships were propelled by a combination of sail and oars. They were made of overlapping planks with a steering oar or board, on the right side, hence the term 'steerboard', or 'starboard'.

AHEAD OF THEIR TIME

Medieval clockmakers were amongst the most skilled craftsmen of their time, at the forefront of technology. The advances they achieved in fine machinery made possible many of today's mechanical machines and engineering feats.

RELIGION

The Church was seen as a stabilising influence in the Middle Ages. But it became too powerful, holding vast estates and accumulating great wealth, leading to inevitable conflict with the Crown. The Church saw its role as civilising a restless society, and it did so largely by fear. Most people went to church as part of their everyday lives; those who did not follow God's word could certainly expect retribution. Although not actually creating the concept of Heaven and Hell, the Church authorities did much to exploit it. In stark contrast, monasteries became centres of art, medicine and learning.

THE DEVIL'S WORK

The Church used dramatic imagery to influence ordinary people. By promoting horrific images of Hell and preying on superstition, many were persuaded to lead righteous lives.

THOMAS BECKET

This picture shows Thomas Becket flouting royal power. As Chancellor, he became Henry II's friend and ally, but on becoming Archbishop he staunchly resisted the King's demands. Becket was murdered in Canterbury Cathedral in 1170 following his return from exile, and was made a saint three years later.

THE WHEEL OF FORTUNE

Those living virtuous lives would be rewarded
on their deaths by entering the Kingdom of God.
The wheel of life always turned full
circle and there was no escaping
judgement for your sins.

THE GLORY OF GOD

Churches are
the most obvious
survivors of medieval
religious zeal. Over 9,000
parish churches and over 300 cathedrals
and monasteries survive as testament
to the religious fervour of the period.

THE CRUSADER KING

Richard I spent only six months
of his reign in England. He took part
in the Third Crusade to the Holy
Land, attempting to liberate Jerusalem.
Generally regarded as a righteous king,
he was in fact a brutal soldier with scant
regard for the Church.

SANCTUARY

In England a fugitive from justice might
claim the sanctuary of a church building.
There he could confess his crime and
renounce his country, without fear of
arrest as he made his way into exile.

RELIGIOUS PERSECUTION

Jews were only allowed
to remain in England if
they served the king.
They were persecuted as
being anti-Christian and
compelled to wear two
strips of yellow cloth
as a "badge of shame".

A GLOSSARY OF MEDIEVAL TERMS

COMMON LAND Contrary to popular belief, common land had never been freely accessible to the general public. It was simply a tract of land (usually the least productive) used "in common" by two or more people. In the Middle Ages it was owned by the lord, who gave his tenants the right to use it.

FELONY Felonies in medieval times were serious crimes punishable by death. Unfortunately, a felony also included, along with murder, the theft of any amount over one shilling!

FORESTS From Norman times, nearly one quarter of England came under "forest law". Forests were vast tracts of land used by the king and his nobles as hunting preserves. The land did not always have tree cover, but as much of it did the word "forest" has come to be associated with dense woodland.

"HAND OF GLORY" Medieval medicine relied heavily on superstition. It was believed that if a cancer sufferer rubbed the affected part of their body with a dead woman's hand (the 'Hand of Glory') they would be cured.

SCOT-FREE A tax known as "Scot" was levied on inhabitants of low-lying marsh areas to pay for the cost of land drainage. Those living on higher ground, who did not directly benefit, were exempt from the tax and so got off "Scot-free", hence the term used today.

STARBOARD Early medieval ships used oars to aid propulsion, with a steering board, or oar on the right side, hence 'Steerboard', which became abbreviated to 'Starboard', still used to define the right-hand side of a ship.

ACKNOWLEDGEMENTS

Medieval Life was published in association with The Bodleian Library, Oxford
We would like to thank: Liz Rowe, Graham Rich, Tracey Pennington and Peter Done
Copyright © 2003 ticktock Entertainment Ltd.
First published in Great Britain by Addax Retail Publishing Ltd., Great Britain. All rights reserved. No part of this publication may be reproduced, stored in a retrieval system, or transmitted in any form or by any means, electronic, mechanical, photocopying, recording or otherwise, without prior written permission of the copyright owner.

Printed in Egypt
Picture credits (Abbreviations: t= top; b= bottom; c= centre; l= left; r= right)
© Angelo Hornack Library; 8-9ct. Anthony Blake Photo Library/ Paul Grater; 10tl. Avoncroft Museum of Historic Buildings, Bromsgrove, Worcestershire; 17br. Bibliotheque Nationale, Paris/ Bridgeman Art Library, London; 21tl, 23ct. Bodleian Library; OFCtl (Roll174D. frame 9), OFCc (174D.4), OBCtl (218.1.4), OBCtr (162B.2.9), OBCcr (164B.1), OBCbr (170H.8), IFC-1 (162B.2.3), IBC (163.3.8), 2tl (173B.9), 2-3c (162.2.12), 3tr (79E.4), 3cr (173B.8), 3cb (162B.2.10), 4tl (164E.5), 5c (164E.7), 6tl (79E.8), 7tr (79E.9), 7cl (145C.15), 7cr (218.1.6), 7bl (173B.2), 8bl (162B.2), 8br (145C.11), 9bl (174D.5), 10ct (145C.2), 11tl (145C.10), 11ct (145C.1), 11cr (MS.Rawl.G.98.fol.49v), 12bl (218.1.13), 12-13c (162B.2.1), 13bl (164D.9), 14tr (164B.1), 14bl (164B.5), 14cb (164B.4), 14br (MS.Bodley.264.fol.181.verso), 15cr (173B.4), 15br (164B.8), 16bl (218.1.10), 18br (170H.3), 17-18ct (170H.9), 19tr (79E.3), 19c (170H.5), 19cl (170H.8), 19cb (79E.6), 20tl (281.1.3), 21cl (218.1.4), 21cr (174D.7) , 21br (218.1.12), 22cl (162B.2.9), 22-23ct (162B.2.8), 24bl (287.2.2), 25tr (164D.2), 25br (164D.8), 26tr (174D.9), 27tr (162B.2.14), 27cr (164B.9), 27br (164B.7), 28-29ct (164E.1), 29br (164B.6), 30cl (218.9.6), 30-31ct (174D.4), By permission of The British Library; 2b, 7br, 31cb. British Library, London/Bridgeman Art Library, London; 3c, 5cb, 20c, 21tr, 26cb, 27cl, 28b, 31cl. British Museum, London/Bridgeman Art Library, London; 15c. C.A. Henley/Biofotos; OFCbl, 4-5t. The Governing Body of Christ Church, Oxford; OFCr, 23r.The Dean and Chapter of Durham; 31ct. Mary Evans Picture Library; 12tl, 24-25ct, 28-29cb, 29tl, 29tr. Musée Conde, Chantilly/Giraudon/Bridgeman Art Library, London; 9tr. Museum of London; OFCbc, OFCct, 5ct, 7-8c, 8tl, 11tr, 14-15c. National Trust Photographic Library/Alasdair Ogilvie; 16-17c. Wellcome Institute Library, London; 22c. Woodmansterne; 9cr, 17ct, 31r.

Every effort has been made to trace the copyright holders and we apologise in advance for any unintentional omissions. We would be pleased to insert the appropriate acknowledgement in any subsequent edition of this publication.

A CIP catalogue record for this book is available from the British Library. ISBN 1 8007 404 9

snapping-turtle
guide